Become a
BIG PICTURE THINKER

Become a
BIG PICTURE THINKER

Learn How To Think Big

EMILY NIGHTINGALE

Copyright © 2018 by Emily J. Garrett
All rights reserved.

This book or parts thereof may not be reproduced in any form, stored
in any retrieval system, or transmitted in any form by any means —
electronic, mechanical, photocopy, recording, or otherwise —
without
prior written permission of the publisher, except as provided by
United States of America copyright law.

For permission requests write to the publisher at
info@hundredacrepress.com.

This is a work of non-fiction but it includes some fictional passages.
It is purely based on the author's opinions. Any names, characters,
businesses, places, events, and incidents are either the products
of the author's imagination, or used in a fictitious manner. Any
resemblance to actual persons, living, or dead, or to actual events, is
purely coincidental.
No liability is assumed for losses or damages due to the information
provided. You are responsible for your own choices, actions,
and results.

Any books and videos referenced, company names, trademarks,
trade names, and product names appearing in this publication are
the property of their respective owners, and the author does not lay
any claim to them.

Ebook ISBN: 978-0-9991198-2-2
Paperback ISBN: 978-0-9991198-3-9

For further information, please contact the author at
emily@emilynightingaleauthor.com

Or visit: www.emilynightingaleauthor.com

Contents

WHAT IS BIG PICTURE THINKING   1
    Introduction   1
    Advantages of Big Picture Thinking   2
    The Lens of a Thought Leader   5
    Famous BPTs   7
    What Kind of Thinker Are You?   15
    Early Brain Training   19
    How does Big Picture Thinking work?   25

FOUNDATION FOR BPTS   29
    Embrace Thinking Differently   29
    Adopt Optimism   31
    Exercise your Brain   33
    Become a Pattern Watcher   37
    Point of View   38
    Focused Thinking   42
    Become a Keen Observer   43
    Lifelong Learning   47

Listen to your Inner Self	47
Hanging Out	49
APPLY BIG PICTURE THINKING SKILLS	**51**
The Process	51
The Why	54
Visualize	56
Organize	57
Analyze	61
Explore	61
Imagine	63
Persevere	64
Your Training in a Nutshell	66
OTHER BOOKS AND COURSES BY EMILY NIGHTINGALE	**71**
REVIEW REQUEST	**73**
BIBLIOGRAPHY	**75**

Become a
BIG PICTURE THINKER

What is Big Picture Thinking

Introduction

WHEN I WAS a kid and people asked me what I wanted to be when I grew up, I always told them I wanted to be a giraffe. Giraffes have continually caught my attention throughout my life. They have a big picture view of everything around them and can move swiftly with their long legs to see whatever is going on and how everything is connected. I always wanted that, too. They can see from far away when a lion is headed in their direction. This gives them plenty of time to adjust their direction to avoid it. With the physical advantage of their great height, giraffes have an opportunity to become the Big Picture Thinkers of the animal world.

In the human world, Big Picture Thinkers are game changers. They are the problem solvers of the world.

They think "outside the box." They are able to envision a future outcome, and then determine what needs to take place to make it happen.

Big Picture Thinking is the way you look at a situation, a problem, or your environment. Whether you are an innovator, or a leader of people or thoughts, Big Picture Thinking can make you more effective. Leaders need to be able to see all the parts and how they fit together. You must always be aware of the "what" and the "why" and whether you are heading toward the goal. When you see clearly what is working well, and what isn't working, you can make necessary adjustments at the right time.

You may already have started to do some Big Picture Thinking and recognize its potential, or know someone who thinks big. In this book, you'll learn more about the advantages of Big Picture Thinking for planning, problem solving, inventing new products, or improving the world around you. You'll also discover how to identify your own thinking type, and the steps you can take to become more proficient in the completion and implementation of your ideas. We'll also discuss some inspirational Big Picture Thinkers and their experiences. After reading this book, I hope you will continue with the concepts introduced to train yourself to be an effective Big Picture Thinker.

Advantages of Big Picture Thinking

BIG PICTURE THINKING is an important skill to learn, whether or not you are a leader. A visual image of the present and the future helps you become more motivated and focused, and therefore, more successful. Big Picture Thinkers have insight into timing, and it helps them make the correct decisions at the right time.

Without a vision of where your team or company or life is headed, there is no way to accurately determine which actions will keep you heading toward a successful destination. Knowing the big picture about your company's mission and the team's goals can help you generate ideas that can help the team move forward, and also motivate you and your team to do routine or boring tasks without complaint.

Imagine the person installing the brakes on a car assembly line. This could be a tedious task to perform all day long. Knowing how important good brakes are to the customer that will one day drive this car, and the probability that it will likely save that person from harm many times can help motivate the worker to do the best job possible. If you are the worker that installs those brakes over and over each day, you might also be motivated to think of a more efficient way to do the installation.

That would make you an Idea Person, but not necessarily a Thought Leader. A typical leader leads people or ideas, or sometimes both. If you are leading ideas, it's easier if you also have the power to make the necessary decisions and employ the necessary resources to carry out your vision. If you are an Idea Person, it can be a disadvantage not to be in a leadership position, as it can become very frustrating to see your ideas squashed over and over because the leaders don't see your vision. (This can sometimes drive people to start their own businesses.)

Let's say that Joe, the worker installing the brakes on cars, has a great idea for improvement, and the supervisor doesn't really understand how Joe's idea is going to be more efficient, and therefore shuts down his idea. Joe becomes frustrated doing it the same way over and over, knowing there is a better way and that no one will listen to him.

Three years pass and then Joe gets promoted into a leadership position. At this point, he is in a position to make the change to the installation process that he had once suggested. Upper management is now ecstatic, because they are saving time and money. The brakes are being installed accurately and twice as fast. A manager remarks about how great the new process is and how much time and money they are saving. Joe is thinking to himself that this change could have happened three years ago, if someone would have listened to him.

A Thought Leader is a go-to person in a field of expertise. It turns out that Joe had the potential to become a Thought Leader, but was not in a position to do so because his supervisor was not a Big Picture Thinker and could not see his potential or the potential of his idea. A Thought Leader generates innovative ideas, AND is able to turn ideas into reality. Now that Joe is in a leadership position and has turned one idea into reality, he is much more likely to do it again. Upper management has recognized his potential, and verified the worthiness of his innovative idea. They are more likely to listen to his next idea.

The Lens of a Thought Leader

A THOUGHT LEADER is a trusted source that motivates and inspires others. An effective leader creates a vision of the future, and then inspires and motivates others to engage and contribute to the delivery of the vision. As a company CTO (Chief Technology Officer) once told my team, "Our mission is to find out what's possible, create what we need, and then create a process for others to follow. Then we move on to something else, and do this again and again." The vision can be as simply stated as this one, and still be clear enough. If you can simplify the vision into a key message for others to follow, they will be able to make corrections around any obstacles, and stay on the path.

The Big Picture vision is an outside view of the landscape, taking all points of view and trends into consideration. Have you ever heard of people that claim to have had outer-body experiences during surgery, where they say they floated up to the ceiling in the room, saw themselves laying on the operating table, and watched the surgeons work on them? Big Picture Thinking is something like that, but not as weird.

Taking a few steps away, your perspective changes to see the patterns of what is going on around you. When you are immersed in the weeds, it's difficult to see what else is happening. When I reference the "weeds" in your environment, I am talking about all of the smaller details. This could be people, processes, physical space, or anything that is part of something larger. What connects them, and what is similar or different? When you look at everything from only inside the weeds, you miss the big picture. Big Picture Thinkers realize that a world goes on outside of their personal bubbles, and they have a burning desire to know more about it.

Remember the Crow's Nest on ships? The Crow's Nest was a basket or a barrel used as a lookout point located in the upper part of the main mast of the ship. Someone was stationed up there to spot approaching hazards, land, other ships, or sometimes icebergs. To get the scope of a situation, you need to envision things from the "Crow's Nest" view. Back before radar was invented, this *was* the only big picture view for a ship. Radar offers that view now for ships, without having to climb up to the mast and fight off crows, but it's still not a bad idea to get someone to climb up and physically look around. This is what we are going to discuss... how to see from the view of the crow and the giraffe.

An example of when I physically could see a situation from the Crow's Nest view is when I was trying to figure out how my tennis doubles partner and I could play better together. I was trying to observe what went wrong whenever we missed a shot, and it was difficult to do while we were on the court playing. Then one day during a tournament, I was up on the observation deck that looked down over the court, similar to the Crow's Nest view. I could easily see the patterns of how the players were playing and it was suddenly easy to spot what they should have done and what went well!

We often take the Big Picture Thinking of others for granted, especially when people have invented fundamental things that are part of our daily lives or have been catalysts to historical change. We don't usually stop to realize how amazing these changes were, or how much effort and planning went into them. Let's take a look at a few examples of some famous BPTs (Big Picture Thinkers) in history who have changed the circumstances of our lives today.

Famous BPTs

⌘ ⌘ ⌘

Thomas Jefferson

⌘ ⌘ ⌘

ONE OF MY FAVORITE examples of a BPT is Thomas Jefferson. This may be because I lived in Virginia for a number of years, and I visited his Monticello home a few times. I wasn't all that fascinated by history in general at the time, but touring his home and hearing about his life had a lasting impression on me. Jefferson's lifestyle was similar in many ways to others in the era in which he lived. He was not perfect and no one ever is. He made mistakes like anyone else, and was similar in many ways to other men of his era. Everyone has strengths and weaknesses, and so did Jefferson.

However, one of his great strengths was Big Picture Thinking. Why was Jefferson a Big Picture Thinker? To be a BPT, you need to be able to see outside of your surroundings, and envision possibilities and trends. He was not only a leader of people, but also a Thought Leader. Thomas Jefferson was in the right time and place for a great opportunity to make a difference. But in order to take advantage of this opportunity, he had to be able to see beyond what existed, and to envision what could be.

Jefferson drafted the Declaration of Independence in 1776. This document proclaimed the independence of the 13 American colonies from Britain, and established universal liberties for all Americans. When looking back at history and assessing the significance of what someone did, you always have to consider the conditions of the environment at that time to fully appreciate it.

Jefferson was the first Secretary of State, and also served two terms as President of the United States. There were no planes, jets, or cars at that time, so just from the aspect of travel you can see that the rigors of these positions were quite different in that era. When Jefferson was President of the United States, it took nearly a week to travel from his home in Charlottesville to the capitol in Philadelphia. This must have provided him plenty of time to think and plan. He was also not distracted by television, video games, or social media.

Jefferson also played a key role in the development of America. He laid the foundation for free public schools, formed the Library of Congress, and founded the University of Virginia. He not only founded the University, but he also designed the buildings, planned the curriculum and served as the first rector. I'm sometimes amazed at the things he accomplished.

Jefferson also had a vision for America to grow from the original 13 colonies to encompass the rest of the land from the Atlantic to the Pacific Ocean. He arranged the Louisiana Purchase from France during his first term as president. He wanted to learn more about the geography of the territory that surrounded the colonies, and that he envisioned would eventually become the United States. He hired the famous Lewis and Clark to do some exploring and learn more about the big picture.

Thomas Jefferson's home in Charlottesville, Virginia, houses many of his inventions. At Monticello, you can see the Great Clock, the first indoor plumbing, a dumb waiter, a hideaway bed, a copy machine, and many more of his inventions. It's sometimes difficult for me to imagine how one person could have so many achievements in one lifetime. Building Monticello or the University of Virginia wasn't as easy as it would be now. He couldn't hire people with college degrees to help him plan it, and then order materials from the local building supply store. He had to have some of the materials, such as glass for the windows, brought over from Europe.

As mentioned earlier, Big Picture Thinking is the way you look at a situation, a problem, or your environment. Jefferson didn't settle for just becoming independent from Britain. He had a vision in his mind of how great this new nation could become, and felt that it was possible to make this all happen. What if Jefferson had settled for breaking away from Britain, built a little log cabin, and went fishing everyday for the rest of his life? If he only considered his own point of view and current personal needs, none of this would have taken place. When you look at everything only from the weeds, you miss the big picture. I'm really glad he didn't choose an alternative path. What would the United States have become without Jefferson's Big Picture Thinking?

Thomas Edison

ANOTHER FAMOUS BPT was inventor Thomas Edison. He was also not only a Thought Leader, but a leader of people. Edison held over 2,000 patents worldwide, and invented about 15 significant inventions that have changed our lives. These include the phonograph, commercially viable electric light, carbon telephone, electric generator, electric lighting system, and more...

I find it difficult to imagine life without these things. However, at the time, there were people who did not think some of these things were necessary or wanted. Some folks thought that the brightness of electric lights was annoying. Edison had to look past other people's opinions and trust his own perception of his vision of the future, just as other Big Picture Thinkers have done, when they envisioned radio, television, computers, and smartphones. Edison relied on dozens of smart people to build and test his ideas. He paid them wages, but they worked hard for him because they, too, were passionate about their work. They sometimes worked very long hours on his projects.

Edison and Henry Ford, another well-known BPT, shared an estate in Fort Myers, Florida, where they spent their winters. I can picture the two of them sitting on the bench looking out over the Caloosahatchee River, sharing their big picture visions of the future. They first imagined the possibilities, and then charted paths to get there.

In 1927, Edison, Ford, and Harvey Firestone had a vision to grow rubber in the United States to supply it to the automobile industry for tires. They thought it would solve a lot of problems for their businesses. They chipped in together to start a botanical research lab. Edison planted thousands of exotic plants and trees and there is still a rubber tree on the estate. Whenever I think about what these guys have done, I realize how much more a Big Picture Thinker could really accomplish.

✕ ✕ ✕

Leonardo da Vinci

✕ ✕ ✕

BORN IN 1452, Leonardo da Vinci was credited with being one of the greatest painters of all time. You may remember him as the artist who painted the Mona Lisa. He also has been considered by some to be the father of paleontology and architecture. He created flying machines, the helicopter, armored vehicles, and methods to implement solar power. Da Vinci also spent time in all of these other endeavors: he did some sculpting, science, music, cartology (drawing maps does require seeing the view from a distance), mathematics and engineering, anatomy, geology, writing and literature, astronomy, botany, and history.

He is thought to be one of the most diversely talented people that ever lived. Some others who are among his diversely talented peers are Benjamin Franklin, Isaac Asimov, Paul Robeson, Dr. Albert Schweitzer, and Aristotle.

Becoming a BPT isn't just for inventors. I use some of them as examples, because inventors are great at connecting concepts and ideas that exist and making something new of them. This can be a product, a company, a process, or just about anything else.

※ ※ ※

Martin Luther King, Jr.

※ ※ ※

I COULD NAME dozens of people in history who have thought in big ways outside of their own personal bubbles and put themselves out there to help their fellow humans. There are other ways to think about the big picture besides inventing items that change the way we live, like the light bulb, rubber tires, or starting a new country.

Reverend Dr. Martin Luther King, Jr. had a vision of changing and improving the way people are treated. He had a vision of an improved future on a massive scale. A Baptist Minister and Civil Rights activist, Dr. King used his Big Picture Thinking to imagine a better world for millions of people. It was his passion for the vision that helped him lead a movement that changed society for the good. He could see in his mind's eye how much better it could be if people were treated equally and fairly. This helped drive him towards the goal. He was the most visible spokesperson for this movement and he won the Nobel Peace Prize in 1964 for combating racial inequality through peaceful protest.

As with Thomas Edison, many people didn't understand Dr. King's vision. When he was president of the Southern Christian Leadership Conference (SCLC), some of his efforts to be involved in the changes about which he was so passionate were fundamentally opposed by other organizations that wanted the same result, such as the Student Nonviolent Coordinating Committee. The SNCC was a major Civil Rights Movement organization in the 1960s, which had different ideas about how to go about initiating this same change.

This happens sometimes—people that agree on a vision have different ideas of how to approach it. (This happened in a similar fashion during the Women's Suffrage Movement between Susan B. Anthony and Lucy Stone. People that share your vision sometimes don't agree upon the steps to get there. You have to know the big picture and the key goal, as they will challenge you re-think and verify your plan.) Dr. King expanded his passion to include poverty and the Vietnam War, and he persevered even while he became an object of an FBI project aimed at discrediting and disrupting his efforts.

※ ※ ※

Big picture thinking, big ideas, grand efforts, and a large amount of passion and perseverance drove these BPTs to accomplish amazing changes that altered the future for the rest of us. Hopefully you are even more inspired after reading a bit about these famous Big Picture Thinkers. Now let's talk about you.

What Kind of Thinker Are You?

THERE IS A school of thought that there are right-brained and left-brained thinkers. In reality, we all use both sides of our brains. Each side of the brain is specialized in different and highly complex modes of thinking, and both sides perform high-level cognitive functions. The communication between the two sides via the corpus callosum integrates the two different ways of thinking the same thought. The connection through this network of nerves between the two hemispheres allows them to work together in a complementary fashion.

The right-hemisphere of your brain processes images, music, emotions, and color. It also handles spatial information and visual comprehension. People that are called right-brained are often artistic, unorganized, intuitive, and innovative. Using the right hemisphere of the brain, you can see how things exist in space and how parts go together to make up the whole. This is where we use intuition and insight to understand images, combine ideas, and build complex thoughts.

Take a look at the following figure. Can you see that a strong right-brain is significant to imagining the vision, and a strong left-brain is significant to completing, communicating and implementing the vision?

LEFT	RIGHT
Math	Images
Language	Music
Logic	Emotions
Critical Thinking	Color
Reason	Shapes

People with a more dominant left-brain are thought to be more logical and objective thinkers. They are usually good with math, language, critical thinking and reasoning. The left-brain is usually the default side of the brain. It often criticizes and judges the ideas that the right-brain imagines. Sometimes those ideas never have a chance, because the left-brain shuts them down before they can be verbalized or written down. The right-brain idea by itself may lack logic and reasoning necessary to complete the picture. Strengthening of the key skills of both hemispheres of the brain is necessary to finalize and implement those ideas successfully.

Although everyone actually uses both sides of the brain, one side can seem more dominant for most people. Which side is more dominant for you? Are you a right-brain or left-brain dominant thinker?

You might be a more right-brained thinker if you:

- Feel disorganized or that organizing your life requires a lot of effort.
- Have lots of great ideas.
- Love to begin new projects.
- Hate details and prescribed tasks.
- Find yourself working on a lot of different things.
- Notice patterns everywhere you look.
- Are not surprised when big changes occur.
- Have too many projects going on at the same time.
- Lose things.
- Are forgetful.

There is nothing wrong with being a right-brain dominant thinker, although you may be frustrated at times when people don't see what you see, and you may have trouble turning your ideas into concrete actions. We need your ideas and your visions!

You might be a more left-brained thinker if some of these descriptions sound like you:

- You love production-type activities and spreadsheets.
- You liked to keep your room clean as a child.
- You are good at test-taking and reading directions.
- You like computers and data or financial analysis.
- You don't like starting big projects.
- You like getting involved in projects with other people, to help solve some of the details of their plans.
- You sometimes experience difficulty prioritizing tasks and activities.
- You just want your boss to tell you exactly what to do.
- Things happen that surprise you, and you realize later that there were clues you missed.

There is nothing wrong with being a left-brain dominant thinker, either! We need you! Details are important, but how do you know which ones are important? You have to know the Big Picture in order to prioritize the details.

Maybe you found yourself in both lists, and have a good balance in your thinking. If that is the case, this process will likely be easier for you. If you have a dominant right-brain, you may have a natural potential for BPT visualization and ideas, but it's the complementary connection between the hemispheres that is key to completing the vision and implementing them successfully.

Early Brain Training

AN ADVANTAGE OF the century in which we currently live is that school attendance is mandatory for all children in many countries. The teaching methods and processes, however, have traditionally lumped all students together in their learning methods, which is a disadvantage for many of them. Since the left hemisphere is where language and logic are housed, it makes sense that in traditional education the system has relied on teaching skills to this side of the brain. However, since the right hemisphere isn't involved in this process, the exercise needed to cultivate ideas and visions is often neglected during the school years (except maybe at recess). Furthermore, it is difficult to grade the type of thinking that is expressed from the right hemisphere, as it is purely subjective on the part of the person doing the grading.

As the educational system evolves, more discoveries are being made about individual differences, and therefore more changes are being made to try to address some of these differences. Back in the early days, there was an advantage for children with dominant right-brains to serve apprenticeships or to follow their own curiosity and interests, rather than sitting in a classroom. This may have been a key to the success of people like Leonardo da Vinci.

Students today don't get many opportunities to follow their passions in school studies until college. The parts-to-whole teaching method has been traditionally employed in the modern educational system, as it is easier to piece out information and test students on their understanding this way. Think about how much standardized testing plays a role in today's education, and how little it has to do with an individual's passion or creativity.

It is a bit challenging to grow up in the traditional school instructional environment for right-brain dominant people. They may struggle to absorb the pieces of learning in the parts-to-whole method without first understanding the goal (Big Picture) of what is being taught. At least that's how they taught us when I was in school.

PARTS TO WHOLE TEACHING METHOD

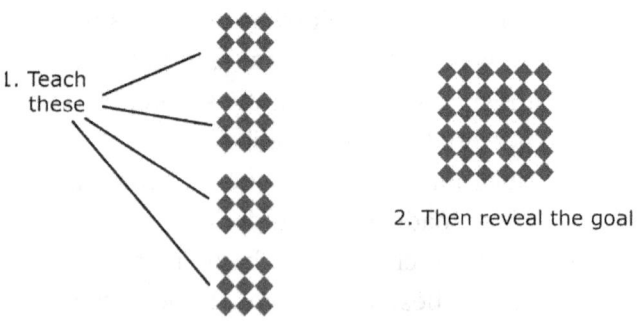

However, in adult education, the whole-to-parts method of teaching is frequently used. They first provide the goal (Big Picture), and the reason you should want to learn about it, and *then* they feed you the pieces of learning. I guess most adults won't do the work without understanding the importance of the goal, whereas children in school don't have a choice.

WHOLE TO PARTS TEACHING METHOD

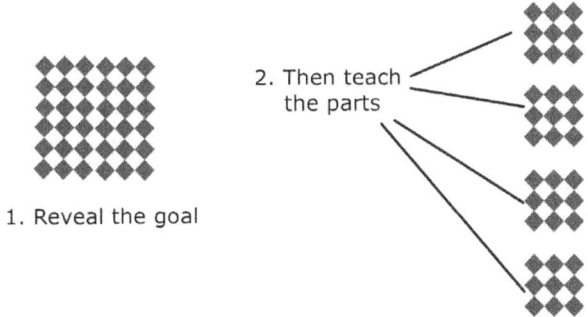

1. Reveal the goal
2. Then teach the parts

Our famous BPTs didn't sail effortlessly to success, either. They, too, struggled at times to get their ideas implemented. Some of them struggled more than others. Albert Einstein was thought to be stupid, perhaps because the creative, innovative side of his brain was so dominant. He was known to have little to say in his early years, and some difficulty speaking until later in his childhood. (Language skills reside in the left hemisphere of the brain.) Author Thomas Sowell wrote that many brilliant people were late in developing speech. Perhaps Einstein didn't think in words. Maybe he thought in shapes and lines and colors instead? I don't know. But when someone who thinks differently is judged by the standards of an average person, the judgment is often incorrect, as in this case.

Thomas Edison was easily distracted in school and his teacher said he was "difficult." His mother pulled him out of school and provided books on everything that interested him. This genius was allowed to follow his passion and became proficient at teaching himself whatever he found interesting.

As you can see, it wasn't always easy for Einstein or Edison. They had curiosity, ideas, and their own methods of observation and discovery. Communicating their ideas and getting people to recognize the value of their ideas took some effort, but they eventually succeeded at this. You can too.

Perhaps because of the time in which Leonardo da Vinci lived (the 1400s), he was not in a situation where his potential was judged by others too soon, as it was with Edison and Einstein. He was able to create what he wanted, prove his idea, and then share it with the world. The vast diversity of da Vinci's interests must have engaged all areas of his brain. In order to imagine and then conjure his ideas into reality, he was apparently able to connect the two hemispheres of his brain in a complementary fashion. Over and over again I see this pattern with successful BPTs.

While one side may dominate strongly, both sides of the brain work together to process ideas, and apply logic to them. You need both sides to process complete thoughts and the language to communicate them. You may have been born with a dominant side, but you can develop the skills needed to strengthen the skills on other side. There are many connections from one side to the other that help the two sides work together. Strengthening this connection is important for big picture thinking.

I didn't even know when I was younger that I had a dominant right-brain. I loved art, never could find my crayons as a child or my keys as an adult, and was extremely unorganized. In fact, I grew to despise looking for items I had lost so much that I taught my right-brained kids a process that uses visualization to find lost items, so that I wouldn't have to help them look for their stuff. As an adult, I quickly realized why my mother had a place for everything and everything in its place. It was because she also was right-brained, and had become spatially organized, just as I eventually would do. I know where everything is, as long as you don't try to put it all away. Things that are put away are in categories. I bank this way, too, with an account for each category.

In college, I somehow ended up in a computer programming degree program at first. I felt like I was sent there, as I had limited options at the time. Looking back, my choice to learn computer programming was a blessing. It requires you to see things from the big picture perspective, but also requires quite a bit of detailed, logical thinking. This was so important to the development of my thinking.

When we were learning the logical steps needed in a computer program: Start with A, then B, and only then you can get to C, it was an eye opening moment for me. It changed my life. I felt like my left-brain started to wake up, and I could see that I'll never get to C, without doing B. This may sound dumb to you if you have a dominant left-brain, but learning logic was a revelation for me. Those connections started happening with the two sides of my brain. You have to think creatively and see the big picture to be an efficient programmer, but you have to employ logic to make it work, so it was a great beginning path for me. By the time I earned my computer programming degree, I was applying logic to my life in a new way. My left-brain was working with my right-brain in a way that it never had before. I had learned to take the big picture, apply logic, and think through the details.

Your perception of the world from both sides of the brain are important. Just because you were born with one dominant side of your brain, doesn't mean you can't strengthen the other side. Having the two sides working together is ideal, and I think necessary for a BPT. There is a theory that the dominant side of your brain switches back in forth in a rhythmic fashion many times in a day, and this is tied to your nostrils. When your left nostril feels more open, your right brain is more dominant, and when your right nostril feels more open, your left-brain is in control. Maybe this is why when I have a head cold, I feel like I can't think at all!

Both sides of your brain are involved in most tasks, but one is always dominant at any given moment in time. The components of the big picture that your right brain perceives are organized and catalogued by your left-brain into logical sequences and labeled. Once you have allowed the left-brain to do its job, it becomes the dominating side and your right brain has trouble expanding your ideas until you find a way to make it dominant again. Integration of both hemispheres helps you learn better, see the long view down the road, think of ideas and solutions, and turn those ideas and solutions into reality.

Let's look at some of the things that BPTs do well, such as patterns and ideas. Then we'll explore some things you can do to become one of them.

How does Big Picture Thinking work?

BIG PICTURE THINKING is mostly about understanding and observing how things are working as units and patterns. Everything in our lives is a pattern of predictable cycles and rhythms. Big Picture Thinkers pay attention to them and take advantage of patterns that already exist. One example is the seasons. Every year we have somewhat predictable seasons of Spring, Summer, Fall and Winter. We can turn on the weather channel and hear them talk about weather patterns, as they predict the weather while it travels across the country and around the world.

Each day we have a pattern of sunrise to sunset. Each month the moon travels a full cycle. The ocean tides are predictable patterns based on the lunar cycle. Electrons revolve around the nucleus of an atom. People study the stock market patterns, farming, behavior, shopping patterns, and even astrology to try to predict the future.

Recognition of patterns has provided the clues needed for BPTs to make great discoveries, such as Nicolaus Copernicus, who developed the concept of a heliocentric solar system. Copernicus was a mathematician and astronomer who revolutionized theories about the solar system. He was called the father of modern astronomy.

Many BPTs, such as Copernicus, did not create new ideas, but discovered new ways to think about or combine old ideas. It was previously believed that the Sun revolved around the Earth. Copernicus developed the concept where the planets revolved around the Sun. He built his own observatory, and created a formula to calculate planetary positions. By studying the patterns, he could test his theories of planetary motion.

Just as some people were against Edison's electric lighting, the church was adamantly against Copernicus' theories for hundreds of years, and banned people from reading his manuscripts or expressing their beliefs in his concept. Copernicus wasn't the first scientist to theorize the planets revolving around the sun. Greek astronomer Aristarchus of Samos had made this same theory hundreds of years earlier, but apparently no one listened to him, either. The church prevailed by refusing to allow anyone to consider these theories. The church had more power than one or two BPTs. As it turned out, Copernicus and Aristarchus were correct.

Copernicus had studied painting and math in school, just as other BPTs of that time had done, such as Leonardo da Vinci. Here again is a pattern of a BPT stimulating both sides of the brain to make the connections needed for big picture ideas, and the logic and critical judgments to develop them and to carry them through to finalize their work. Is it a coincidence that many of the great inventors and theorists studied subjects that used both right and left-brain thinking?

Along came Galileo Galilei, another famous BPT, who was born in 1564. He was a mathematics professor who recognized patterns in our universe that have had long-lasting implications for the study of physics. Galileo was interested in geometry, math, and astronomy, all of which are based on patterns. Since math is quite logical, my guess is that Galileo made full use of the left hemisphere of his brain. However, Galileo's father was a musician, a right-brained profession. Music also teaches us about rhythm and patterns. I imagine growing up in a household with a musician drives home the recognition of patterns consciously and unconsciously. Galileo refined theories on motion and falling objects. He also developed the universal law of acceleration, which is obeyed by all objects in the universe.

Galileo agreed with Copernicus that the Earth and planets revolved around the sun. After learning about the telescope, Galileo made his own telescope, allowing him to learn much more about astronomy. Galileo was threatened with torture by his church for believing that the Earth evolved around the sun, which we all know now that it does. He was placed under house arrest for the rest of his life, and was not supposed to have visitors or share any of his theories in printed works outside of Italy. Luckily for us, he defied this order, and shared his theories, so that we could all benefit from his revelations and knowledge.

BPTs have to be willing to break out of their comfort zones and question conventional thinking when they see patterns that are telling a different story, or when hatching a new idea. The world often does not see the BPT's vision and this often takes time and struggle before they do. BPTs often encounter resistance and ridicule from other people when they are ahead of their time, like Copernicus, Galileo and Edison did. You can't let this slow you down or stop you. This is how it has always been.

Foundation for BPTs

ANYONE CAN BECOME a BPT, but it may be easier for some people than others. It depends upon your starting point. You are probably already doing some of the necessary thinking to become a BPT, which is why you recognized its importance and are reading this book.

An important thing to remember as a Big Picture Thinker is to avoid being a procrastinator. People who procrastinate spend more time thinking about the past than the future, and they waste mind power thinking about the tasks they are putting off. You need to clear your mind of this type of clutter to be an effective BPT.

The following sections outline some of the foundational strengths that are important to develop or strengthen to become a BPT or a more successful BPT.

Embrace Thinking Differently

BPTS EMBRACE THINKING differently, and feel comfortable about not following the crowd, just as our previous examples did. Parents and teachers get frustrated over the child that thinks differently and questions everything. "Please, just do as I ask!" they plead with this child, as the other children politely follow along and do what they are told. The children that follow directions of teachers and parents are praised, and the one that questions everything and thinks differently is often scolded and made to feel wrong.

It's the child that questions and thinks differently that is the most likely to become a BPT (good news for their parents). It's time to shake that feeling that you were wrong for questioning the status quo, and embrace the power to think differently and change the future.

- Do you follow what you are told without question or do you follow your heart and your intuition, when it does not agree with what other people are saying?
- Do you enjoy working in a group with a leader to explain the vision so you can follow it, or do you enjoy contributing to the vision?
- Do you have a larger vision for your career or project?
- Are you working in positions or on projects that are leading somewhere that matters to you?

If you are following your intuition, and questioning and contributing to the vision when you don't quite agree with it, you are on the correct path. Thinking beyond your present project or career status means you are thinking bigger than the present reality. Keep it going!

Adopt Optimism

TO DO YOUR best Big Picture Thinking and to address future possibilities and problem solving, you need to be strongly optimistic. Optimism is the tendency to look favorably on not only the future, but everything that happens to you and in your environment. You would need to ask yourself, "What is the possible positive outcome of this seemingly bad situation? How can I get there?" (Also known as looking on the bright side, or staying on the sunny side of life.)

Negative thinking will quickly shut down your Big Picture Thinking, because when you see obstacles, thinking negatively will shut the door on any ideas before you get close to a solution. How can you possibly expand your thinking while you are contracting your thoughts and feelings? I have always heard that the human brain is wired to lean toward the negative and that you must practice positive thought processes to strengthen those positive connections. So think of it this way if you are struggling with this, you must rewire your thinking and adopt a positive approach to all challenges. Fake it, if necessary, until it feels normal, but do what you must to keep those optimistic neural pathways exercised to make them stronger.

Visualization has been discovered to help athletes become successful. They not only physically practice a sport faithfully, but also add some visualization exercises of successful achievement or mastery of the sport over and over. Just as visualization and physical practice works to master a sport, optimism will get easier with practice.

I discovered the concept of looking for the positive in a situation after an experience when I was a teenager. I was riding in the car with my boyfriend to his house. Obviously, he had traveled to his house many times and shouldn't have consciously needed to think about where to turn to get there. But for some odd reason, he missed his turn. We had to travel several miles before he could turn around and come back. When we reached his street, there had been an accident. Someone had run into the back of a car that was turning onto the same street and pushed the car up into a yard and into someone's house. The police had just arrived and they were preparing to clear the accident from the street.

We realized at the time that if it had not been for our missed turn and the time it took to turn around, that we could have been the car that was hit trying to turn onto that street. Ever since that day, when seemingly bad things or delays happen — a flat tire, a missed call, etc., I look beyond the obvious and look for the good in the situation.

What was the good side of an unwanted situation? How did the delay or missed call help you? I often discover what that was. When I don't, I accept that it exists and that I just don't know what it is yet, or I may never know. I've seen the positive side of seemingly negative situations so many times, that I don't question that there is a positive reason for the way many things happen. Have you ever lost your job and then found a new one that you liked much better? You wouldn't have looked for it, if you hadn't been unemployed.

I know sometimes it's really difficult to look on the bright side when really bad things happen. However, I have often said that the worst things that have happened to me have brought some of the best things into my life, but I can't see this until much later when I look back. If you look back as I have, you may also find that some of the bad things that happened to you opened a door for some of the best things that have happened to you, too.

To maintain a positive outlook, you sometimes have to look beyond the obvious for the good. It's there. If it's not obvious, you'll just have to trust that it's there.

Exercise your Brain

Exercising the Right Brain

YOUR BRAIN HAS many pathways and connections, and your activities and thoughts create and strengthen those pathways and connections. You have control of what happens in your brain by doing these things purposefully. The left hemisphere of the brain is the default side, and it is often judging and shutting down the great ideas that are being conjured in the right hemisphere. This is extremely frustrating, and you don't have to stand for it.

In the book, *Drawing from the Right Side of the Brain*, Betty Edwards has people draw upside down to engage the right side of the brain so it will be in control, and so the left-brain will stay out of the way of their creativity. When you draw upside down, your brain has no idea what the object you are drawing should look like and is unable to judge it. Therefore the left-brain can't find a way to take over. But the right-brain enjoys this abstract-looking creation and engages itself.

If you feel stuck when you are trying to do your Big Picture Thinking, try drawing something upside down to tell your right brain to get in gear. Or do something else in an illogical way. The left-brain expects you to do things in a certain way, so change it up. Do something carefree. Eat something you never eat, dress in a totally different way, brush your hair with your opposite hand, try something new — do something to break your routine that your brain does not expect. Then start writing down all of your thoughts without judging them. Once the judgment begins, it often means that the left hemisphere is back in control, so be careful not to judge while doing a brain dump of ideas.

When my children were in elementary school, I was pleased to see that more right-brained activities had been added. For example, when they did a book report, they had options of whether to create some art or music to present it. The more often your right-hemisphere is involved with your left-hemisphere in learning, the more balanced your cognitive functioning will be, and the easier it is to become a Big Picture Thinker.

Exercising the Left Brain

IF YOU HAVE a dominant right-brain, and need to get your left brain moving, activities like crossword puzzles, brainteasers and logic games, or word problems that are focused on language and mathematic skills will exercise the left hemisphere of your brain. You could also try writing, listening to music or singing. Maybe you would enjoy learning another language. Your left-brain enjoys all of these things. You should be able to find some apps for your phone, or puzzle and brainteaser books to keep on hand when you want to get some left-brain exercise.

My uncle used to do the crossword puzzle in the newspaper every morning, and also look up a random word in the dictionary to learn and use each day. When he was in his eighties, he recited a really long poem to me that he said he had learned in high school. I'm not sure how often he practiced it, but he didn't miss a word.

Integration of Both Sides

PHYSICAL MOVEMENT OF both sides of the body forces the brain to work in an integrated fashion. Walking, crawling, running, and dancing all require rhythmic body parts on both sides of the body, directed by both brain hemispheres. In yoga class, we do a lot of alternating movements, and crossover twisting movements that cross the center or midline of the body. This is supposed to help get our energy flowing through our organs, but also builds pathways in the brain.

You may hear over and over how important playtime is for developing children. If you are a parent, you may have noticed that small children can spend hours with a cardboard box, or some pots and pans, or may be more interested in the bow on a gift, than the gift itself. Playtime develops imagination, which is the right hemisphere of your brain. It also frees you from your normal activities and rules of your life, so it has an important impact.

Some local churches in my area held a program a few years ago to help people become internally stronger, and one of the elements of the program was to regularly plan some time for play. In this crazy, busy world, we are so structured in the things we have to do, that we often don't find time to play in an unstructured manner, as children do so well, or just to do something that is not accomplishing something. If you feel guilty when you spend a little bit of time not achieving something, stop it! You don't have to spend every minute of your life achieving something.

Play is a natural and important element of developing a strong person, and also letting your mind wander and imagine. This is achieving something- a healthy brain! Structured play is great too! Whether you like competitive sports, bike riding, sailing, or building a snowman with the neighborhood kids, play of any kind gets you away from the rules and daily grind and allows your mind to wander. It's a great time for insights and ideas to come to you. Put yourself in the position where insights and ideas will happen and plan some play time each week for yourself.

Become a Pattern Watcher

IDENTIFYING PATTERNS IN your environment helps you determine if something is outside the pattern that you expect. It helps you see connections and cause-and-effect relationships and activities around you.

You can find patterns in many different ways. There are patterns in time, color and sound, cause-and-effect relationships, or the way people or things are connected. This is something you can train yourself to recognize by studying different kinds of patterns.

The mind is a self-organizing system. It passively allows information to sort itself out into categories and store them into memories. Think about the wall of boxes at the Post Office. The mind sorts out the incoming thoughts and categorizes and stores each thought in the correct box, while establishing connections to other memories.

For example, when you were a child your mother always made your favorite blueberry pancakes on Saturday mornings. As an adult, every time you eat blueberry pancakes, you may think about your mom, or Saturday mornings. Every Saturday morning, you may think about your mom and blueberry pancakes. When you are with your mom, you may remember how much you love Saturday mornings and blueberry pancakes.

The effectiveness of the mind comes from its ability to create, store, and recognize patterns. In an experiment using random lines or random sounds, your mind will try to pick out patterns, just as they would in any environment. The good news is that your mind will work with you to allow you to see the patterns presented in your environment. Don't judge the pattern. Just observe and record it. You may not understand it yet. It may be too early or you may not have all the information yet.

Have you ever been in a situation that seemed familiar, and you said to yourself, "I think this kind of thing has happened before?" Sometimes this is because it is a pattern, and if you stop and try to identify when it happened before, you may be able to also remember the outcome, which may help you see the possible outcome of the present situation. It may also give you an opportunity to do something different to change the outcome of the present situation.

Sometimes the impetus for needing to see the big picture in a situation is a change in the pattern.

Point of View

IF YOU ONLY consider your own point of view you won't get very far as a BPT. You must incorporate other points of view in your thinking. When you are Big Picture Thinking about a situation, having empathy for the people involved can help you explore the needs of those people, from their points of view.

Having empathy for others is different than sympathy. Empathy is the ability to understand and share the feelings of another person. Sympathy is when you just feel sorry for them, without necessarily seeing their point of view. Having sympathy for someone else includes feeling compassionate about how someone feels or feeling sorry for them because of some difficulty they are experiencing, and there is nothing wrong with that. But empathy allows you be open to really understand how they feel by putting yourself in their shoes.

Some people are more empathetic than others and may get bogged down by spending too much time in another person's shoes, however, some degree of empathy or measure of being the same person as someone else helps you really understand their current point of view. It also helps you understand how a person's past experiences may influence their responses or decision-making in the present and future.

Sally's brother had a diving accident when he was 15 and she was just 10 years old. He ended up paralyzed from the neck down and was destined to spend the rest of his life in a wheelchair. Sally saw first-hand the difficulties for her brother and her family in navigating stores, buildings, sidewalks, the beach or anywhere and everywhere they went. She was a little surprised with so many disabled people in the world that this was so difficult. Maybe that was the impetus for her becoming an architect.

As an architect, do you think Sally took disabled people into consideration in her building designs? You betcha! She was never in a wheelchair herself, but she wanted people like her brother to become as independent as possible. Sally's empathy for her brother allowed her to see the big picture of what needed to change in the world.

What are some struggles that you see for other people, that you don't experience yourself? How about the older lady working at the corner drugstore? She's so slow and you're in a hurry. She takes so long to put your stuff in a bag. She can hardly stand up straight. You might be thinking — why did they hire her? And the story might be that her husband had died, the insurance ran out, and she was trying to eek out enough to live, as many older people have to do. The hiring manager at the store knew he could count on her to come to work, and do her best, so of course they hired her.

Her point of view is that she feels lucky to have this job so she can pay her bills and she is going to do the best she can at her job. The store manager's point of view is that he can count on her to do what needs to be done and that she will be reliable and she is doing a job that not many people would want. That's the other point of view. You just need to be more patient.

Can you empathize with her or do you just feel sorry for her? Can you put yourself in her shoes and see her point of view?

Thomas Edison was focused on what could improve the quality of life for other people — to serve a need when he passionately experimented and created many of his inventions. Martin Luther King was focused on what could improve life for many other people in a different way — also to serve a need. He had to see the point of view of the people whose life experiences he wanted to improve.

The greater good is a great reason to envision a better future and can drive the passion to make it happen. But Big Picture thinking isn't necessarily about inventing or making something happen, it's just about seeing the vision, the viewpoint—standing back or thinking ahead and trying to see the overall view of a situation with all of its moving parts. When assessing a gap, or working for the greater good, it's important to be able to see other points of view than your own.

Here is another example of empathy and seeing someone else's point of view in a small but impactful way:

When my son, Ben, started kindergarten, his teacher, Mrs. Grogan (not her real name), was in her first year of teaching. The first day five-year-old Ben met her, she had a fuzzy green Kermit the frog © puppet tucked into her belt. She said, "When you look for me, I'll be the teacher with Kermit." She had put herself in the shoes of her kindergarteners and realized that from the eye level of a five-year old, all the teachers look the same! She realized how difficult it would be to distinguish her face from the other teachers from their small stature. She used Kermit to help them easily locate her.

Mrs. Grogan and Kermit greeted her kindergarten class for the first week of every school year for her entire career. Kermit looked pretty worn out the last year before she retired, but he did a great job over the years. I thought it was a brilliant idea. I'm sure that Kermit was just an indicator of Mrs. Grogan's empathy for the children and her attempt to understand their experiences. I'm sure that the children experienced the empathy she had for them many times while they were in her class. All of the children loved her.

Challenge your assumptions by trying to see other people's points of view. Have you ever felt completely wrong about something when someone explained a situation to you? Ask questions, even if you think the answers might challenge you to think differently. Listen to the answers instead of assuming that you already know what the answers are. Discuss your ideas and listen intentionally to other people.

Focused Thinking

BIG PICTURE THINKERS take time to think purposefully and in a focused way.

Getting outside for any reason gets you away from your daily grind and allows you to free your mind a bit. Taking walks, running, and yoga/meditation can help with brainstorming, daydreaming and quieting the noise in your head. Focused thinking is a little different, in that you specifically focus on certain topics and think through them.

As an introvert, my focused thinking time has been extremely important to me. This is something that introverts do more naturally. However, in today's world of distractions, it has become much more difficult for everyone. I know that I don't get enough of it in this busy, distracting world, and I always want more. I often realize I am trying to do too many things, and I end up not getting very far on any one of them. At this point, I have to re-assess my priorities and become more focused on my highest priorities.

You can't just keep working hard and jumping from one thought to another if you want to think BIG. It is important to schedule regular focused thinking time. Some of the topics that are part of your focused thinking time will just show up in your brainstorming and daydreaming.

I do my best, most focused thinking at the beach. However, since I don't live near the beach, it's not frequent enough. Can you spend a day each month or some time each week? Set aside at least a few hours at a time for some focused thinking. Think about places where you are able to think best. Maybe you should pack a lunch and sit in the park. What about sitting at a coffee shop with your computer and writing your thoughts? Close yourself into your home office. Sit on your back porch. Is there a beach nearby? What works best for you? Regular focused thinking time will help you think through some of your observations more deeply. But if you don't plan it, it won't happen. Even if you do plan it, you need to be committed to it to make it work.

Become a Keen Observer

FROM EVERYTHING WE have discussed so far, you should have a pretty good idea of what is involved in Big Picture Thinking. Start with practicing observation. Be a good observer and practice doing observational thinking. Take notes and write down your ideas as they come to you.

Journals are a tool used by Big Picture Thinkers to record their thoughts. You'll be able to look back through your journals to not only remember your insights and ideas, but to see patterns from an objective point of view over time. To help keep your brain in balance, use the left page for notes, and the right page for sketches. It takes many processes in your brain to be a really good observer and to use your senses at their fullest capacity.

There are different ways to observe: passively and actively. If your eyes are open and you can see what is in front of you, you are observing passively. If you are multi-tasking, that is, doing something else while you are looking at what is in front of you, you're not even passively observing. You are not likely to remember anything you saw.

To be a good observer, you must actively observe. Think about how a blind person moves about with a cane. I've heard that a blind person's other senses are more keen, however, it might just be that the other senses are more actively engaged. Do you know how many steps there are from your front door to the sidewalk, or how many paces to your driveway? A blind person is more likely to be aware of the number of steps or paces to get to familiar places, and the location of furniture in the room. They can't fall back on eyesight to let them know these things. They observe without seeing.

When you sit on your front or back porch and listen with your eyes closed, can you identify the different sounds you hear? Did you notice them all when your eyes were open? Paying attention to details, remembering what you saw or heard, and thinking through the logic of what you observed are all skills that you can improve with practice. People are not necessarily born with these skills —they can be developed.

I remember a game we played at my friend Nancy's birthday party in second grade. Her father brought out a tray with about 30 items on it. We had one minute to look at them and then we had to try to remember what was there. Then the tray was taken away, and we had a limited amount of time to write down everything we saw. I won the game. I guess my mind wasn't so cluttered with so many other things at the time because I was so young. This game of observation showed up a few more times throughout my life and I didn't do as well as that first time.

Detectives solve cases by adding up the clues and noticing the puzzle pieces that don't logically add up, or if there are extra clues that didn't fit into the scenario. Being a good observer is extremely important to getting the big picture right.

There are several other ways to improve your observational skills. Besides trying to remember a tray full of items, try walking into the next room and writing down everything that was in the room you just left.

Another way to practice observational skills is to try to reconstruct an event you attended. Did you go to a party last night? Who was there? What were they wearing? Name everything that happened. Or maybe you were in a big meeting at work. Who was there? Who wore a blue shirt? How many people wore jackets? What did they say? What were the important points of the meeting? What was in the room? Who had a laptop? Partner with a friend or spouse and quiz each other on the details of the situation you were just in.

Try meditation. Sitting at your desk at work, close your eyes and think about what you notice in your environment. A ticking clock, a conversation, the hum of a fan, someone typing... This will help strengthen your ability to pay attention and to focus. Meditation is said to improve your brain's activity levels, which will help your ability to observe. You might also try a meditation class.

Try some brain puzzles. Crosswords, cryptograms, brain teasers, and optical illusions will help increase your ability to think logically and notice patterns and look deeper into what is presented.

Have you ever driven to work or home from work and realized you didn't pay attention to anything along the way? If you haven't, then you are not normal. Much of what we do that is repetitive doesn't even register in our brains. The things that are different are the ones that get our attention.

Try doing something different on the way home next time. Try a different route or pull over in the park or the mall and think about what you see. Notice how many people are wearing red shirts. Write down everything you see and wonder about.

Try explaining your travel route to someone else. Where do you turn? What are the street names and landmarks? Are there any businesses along the way? After you have tried to remember all the details, then pay attention next time and notice what things you missed.

Lifelong Learning

STAY OPEN TO opportunities to learn new skills, meet people, and visit places. You can't know the big picture and remain static. The picture changes and you have to keep learning about it.

Study the patterns, study the trends. Think about where things are heading and what is next. Lifelong learning is important for a Big Picture Thinker. Continue to educate yourself and learn about things that take you out of your comfort zone.

Listen to your Inner Self

IF YOU ARE paying attention to the big picture, you are paying attention to your inner hunches and your dreams. Have you ever awakened in the middle of the night with a great idea, but in the morning you forgot it? I have many times. Once I tried writing it down, but when I woke up in the morning, it was just a bunch of scribbles that I couldn't read.

Your subconscious does a lot of great work while you are asleep, and it's a shame when you can't remember it. Always revisit something you are working on after you have had a chance to sleep, because new connections may surface from your subconscious.

I can't stress enough the importance of getting enough sleep. If you want to be a Big Picture Thinker, you need to get to the restorative and dream stages of sleep. Sleep deprived people have trouble focusing. Extra caffeine may help you stay awake, but it does not cure the lack of enough sleep and may (will probably) keep you from focused thinking.

Every once in a while, and for some more than others, we wake up in the morning clearly remembering a dream. These are the ones I try to remember. There are often subconscious clues in dreams that are provided by your brain to you. Once you start your morning routine, the elements of the dream will quickly fade, so write down the dream the very first thing after you wake up and remember it.

Here is one of mine:

I was working for a large company at the time. I had just switched jobs to a different division of the company. I dreamed one night that a tornado had occurred during the night, but it had not affected me, my house, or my family. We looked out the windows in the morning and the sky looked eery and there were huge trees down and devastation all around. We hadn't heard a storm at all, and were quite surprised by it.

I don't usually remember my dreams, but this one was speaking loudly and clearly. I still remember the vivid imagery of that dream from 20 years ago. Living in the Midwest in a tornado prone area, it was a little disturbing. So I looked up the meaning of the dream. The dream dictionary that I referenced said this meant there would be some chaos surrounding me but it would not affect me.

About two months later, there was a large layoff at work. The department I had recently left was dissolved and all of my previous colleagues were given their walking papers, along with a large number of people from that division of the company. Ever since that dream, I always pay attention to a dream that is so vivid. It was too bad that so many people lost jobs, but I was relieved that the premonition dream was not literally about a devastating tornado.

Hanging Out

MOTIVATIONAL SPEAKER JIM Rohn said, "You are the average of the five people with whom you spend the most time."

Who are those five people for you? If you want to work be a better Big Picture Thinker, then spend more time hanging out with other BPTs so that they can influence you. Some of the best ideas flow from conversation. Remember how well that worked for Thomas Edison, Henry Ford, and Harvey Firestone?

Apply Big Picture Thinking Skills

The Process

THE PROCESS AND methods of Big Picture Thinking aren't too surprising. You may be envisioning something new, or you may be stepping back to see the current big picture. The process is very similar in either case.

1. First define the problem to solve, question to be answered, or future vision.
2. Then define what success looks like.
3. Generate a list of circumstances and patterns.
4. Generate a list of questions and answers.
5. List ideas of possible solutions that includes past experiences. Consider similar situations and known solutions, but always include

alternative solutions. This keeps you from limiting yourself to a narrow view and requires you to explore new ideas.
6. Identify resources, including people who might have information or the ability to contribute to the success of the outcome.

Let's walk through the process of a physician back when scientific research was in its early stages. In 1846, Dr. Ignas Semmelweis was an assistant professor at the General Hospital in Vienna and he had a problem to solve. This was an era when physicians were just beginning to turn to science for answers and solutions to illness. They began collecting data and performing autopsies to try to understand why people died.

Semmelweis noticed that in the two maternity wards at the hospital, there were large numbers of women dying of a fever right after childbirth (problem to solve). He began collecting data. He discovered that there were five times as many deaths in the maternity ward staffed by medical students and male doctors, as the ward staffed by midwives. (pattern of the problem)

After experimenting with several theories to no avail, he was frustrated. He began by looking at the obvious differences and changing things around. Then he moved to Big Picture Thinking mode and studied the patterns of the practices of each maternity ward to determine the subtle differences.

At one point, he needed to step back from the situation, as often is needed for Big Picture Thinking, or the Crow's Nest view. He went on vacation to give himself

Apply Big Picture Thinking Skills

more distance and time to think about it — to essentially get out of the weeds. Then, after he had stepped away from it for a bit, a pathologist died from the same illness, and he incorporated this new information into the picture. This is when he came upon the correct solution.

Semmelweis determined that since the doctors and medical students also performed autopsies, there might have been some debris left on their hands. He requested that everyone started washing their hands and rinsing in chlorine, before delivering babies. You see, at the time, germs had not yet been discovered, so he had no scientific evidence to back up his theory. The doctors and medical students didn't wash their hands, if you can imagine that today.

By trial and error, Dr. Semmelweis had concluded correctly that the doctors and medical students lack of hand washing was causing the deaths of the patients. Because germs were not yet discovered, no one believed him. He had found the solution, but he didn't have the germ discovery to back up his solution. They felt he was blaming them for the deaths and did not *want* to believe him. Without scientific evidence to support his findings, it was only the Big Picture Thinking process by Dr. Semmelweiss that enabled him to figure out what was actually happening and discovering the solution to the problem. Big Picture Thinking works well in problem solving, even when proof and scientific verification is not available to provide some of the clues needed. In this case, it would save lives by getting to the root of the problem prior to the discovery of germs, which came years later.

Just like the student who is smarter than his teacher, you can find yourself in a situation where the people around you just don't get it. That's when you may have to break out of your safe zone or start charting a path to a place where you can implement your ideas, even if it means working independently. You wouldn't be the first person to think outside the box, to see something really great out there, and then jump out of the box and make it happen.

You will find many occasions where it doesn't matter if anyone gets the big picture or not, as long as you do. Don't let anything hold you back from Big Picture Thinking — there is no downside to developing this skill. Some BPTs have used this skill to carve out very successful lives for themselves, and others have started billion dollar companies.

I wonder how many real genius inventors are out there that realize that their inventions would blow people's minds if anyone found out about them, so they just don't tell anyone. Just sayin'.

The Why

IN ORDER TO solve a problem or employ a strategy, always begin by imagining the desired outcome (the why). Whatever problem you are trying to solve, or goal you are trying to achieve, keeping the "why" in mind is important absolutely crucial to successful

Apply Big Picture Thinking Skills

Big Picture Thinking. Once you have a vision of what the outcome looks like, you can start to see the steps that need to happen. When you have the big picture in mind, you can see how the day-to-day activities and the opportunities fit into it.

It's an important aspect of success to see the big picture, no matter what job you currently hold. The big picture is not always clear, but if you don't know the desired outcome of a goal, you can be easily led off track. You need to know where you are headed to make sure that your activities and effort are on track.

Embrace change and keep learning what is new about your world. Continual learning keeps you aware of more pieces of the picture, so that you can recognize them. Stay open to opportunities to learn new skills, meet new people, and visit new places. You can't remain static. The picture is always changing and you have to keep learning what is new about it. If things didn't keep changing, we would all be bored out of our minds.

Discuss your ideas and listen intentionally to other people. People love it when other people take an interest in them, and they will often happily provide insight and information that you may need later. Remember, Big Picture Thinkers Henry Ford and Thomas Edison owned winter homes next to one another in Fort Myers, Florida, so that it would be convenient to think together. If you want to be an inspired thinker, take a tour of the Edison Ford Estates and learn more about how Ford and Edison's collaborative thinking contributed to their personal successes. I was surprised to find out just how much Big Picture Thinking and collaboration they were doing!

Albert Einstein and Linus Pauling, another famous scientist, also had a collaborative relationship. They had a personal and professional relationship and spent much time together discussing their thoughts. Pauling was a chemist and activist who won the Nobel Peace prize twice. He kept a journal where he took notes on conversations he had with Einstein. He could refer to his notes whenever he was thinking BIG.

Visualize

MY COLLEAGUE AND I once did an experiment with our team to try to get people to call on the creative side of their brains more readily. We provided everyone with paper and markers, and asked them to draw their résumés in graphic format. Some of them struggled more than others in trying to get away from making lists and using language, indicating that some of them may be more left-brain dominant.

If you haven't seen a graphical résumé, I'd like you to take a moment to look at a few. Using a search engine in your browser, search for "infographic résumé." Then click Images. You should see quite a few of them. Click some of them and take a closer look at some of the images of résumés that are in graphical format to see how the information is arranged and represented. See how different this is than a traditional "language only" résumé? This is an example of a combined right and left-brain created document.

Get out a notebook and try creating your own graphical résumé. This is a great exercise for helping you take data and produce imagery by integrating your right brain. You can just sketch it out with a pencil, but if you are really getting the hang of it, add some color and really try to make it look nice and open those pathways and make those connections.

Organize

THE MIND MAP is a tool similar to the graphical résumé. The Mind Map concept was invented by Tony Buzan. It combines images and words and organizes them into a big picture overview.

Remember how I said the left-brain judges the right-brain's ideas? This often happens when you are trying to write notes or make outlines. This is why Mind Mapping is such a wonderful tool, because it is a visual image of your ideas. You can draw shapes or use just a few words to describe the idea and place them on a page. This helps you get the ideas down and connect them to other ideas, without worrying about the order of things.

I don't know this to be true, but I suspect this is how things looked in Albert Einstein's mind — that he had different images and shapes and moved them around in his mind until he found ways to connect the ideas. Mind mapping is a great way to lay out a problem or goal, while adding in circumstances surrounding the goal, and possible obstructions or solutions. By doing this in a brainstorming fashion where you do not judge what you write, but add things immediately as they occur to you, you are not allowing your left-brain to judge them and thus stomping on the ideas in your right-brain. By documenting all this in a visual way, the problem solving side of your brain can swirl around the elements and help you visualize the big picture, while adding in the weeds (details) to your layout as they occur to you.

The purpose or goal can be big or small. You could be writing a book or movie plot, inventing a new process or product, planning an event, or trying to understand a situation or person. Use your past experience knowledge and observation of the present to lay the groundwork for the big picture.

To create a Mind Map, begin with a large piece of paper and some colored pencils or markers. Draw a shape in the middle of the paper, with a few words to indicate the purpose or goal in the center of the page.

Apply Big Picture Thinking Skills

Draw circles, squares or whatever shape you want on the page with a sketch or words inside to represent the idea. Dump your entire list of ideas out of your mind and on the page in this manner. You can draw arrows from one idea or shape to another to connect any thoughts that should be connected, and don't worry about how it looks. This allows the right-brain to dump its contents (ideas and vision) onto paper without being filtered.

Using different colors and shapes adds to the details, while stimulating the imagination and creativity side of your brain into the activity. By writing down the first ideas that come to your mind about all of the possible scenarios of thought about this topic and future vision, and anything that relates to it, you may be able to get a clearer picture of the situation or topic.

This is important - don't judge your thoughts as you write them down. You are not showing this to anyone. If you judge your thoughts, you will not think freely and you might miss something important. By judging your thoughts, you will have switched out of right-brain mode and into left-brain mode, so be careful not to do this until the appropriate time.

After you have had a chance to step away from your mind map, revisit it and make any additions that come to mind. Once you feel you have everything on the map, get a new sheet of paper, and revise your map to move the elements into a more organized fashion, with the connected elements closer together.

You may want to repeat this process again, depending on the complexity of the goal. Once you have a visual map that is fairly organized, you can begin translating it into either a Context or Concept Map, or into language. A Context or Concept Map puts ideas into context and summarizes the information and connections. For a more complicated idea with a lot of details, a Context Map may be the best way to summarize your ideas in a visual format.

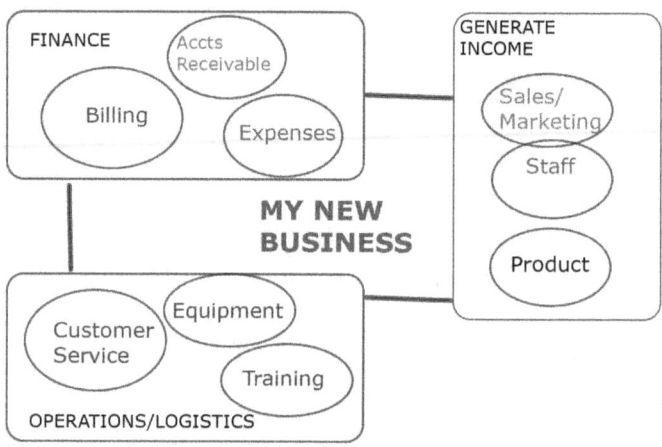

If you are translating this into language, create an outline, beginning with the purpose or goal at the top of the page. Translate all of the ideas on your page into a list, in any order. Just get them translated into words. They should be in pretty good order, since you revised your Mind Map before you started the outline process, but it doesn't matter. This is where the left-brain starts to organize the ideas into language.

You can see how the right and left-brain need to work together to make progress.

Analyze

DEPENDING ON WHAT you are doing, creating the visual Mind Map might be as far as you go with it. By looking at the situation in a visual way, you may see the answer you seek. At this point you could write a hypothesis or two and then do some observation. Compare your scenarios to what you observe to determine if the clues you discover prove any of them to be correct.

If you are doing your Big Picture Thinking as a way of planning something complex, such as starting a business, writing a book, or transforming your department, you may want to take this further and convert this into an outline. Once you have the outline, you can start filling in the details and steps you need to get to the goal. Once you look at your outline, you can identify categories and identify your ideas. What doesn't make sense? What stands out? What have you seen before? You may want to make a few changes and add some things at this point.

Explore

EXPLORE THE POSSIBILITIES of what might be next. Look for emerging patterns and trends.

BECOME A BIG PICTURE THINKER

Years ago I listened to an audio book called *Clicking: 17 Trends That Drive Your Business—And Your Life* by Faith Popcorn. It was published in 1998. This book was about positioning your business and yourself to be poised to take full advantage of the coming trends. And she was spot on with so many trends. One thing that stood out to me at the time was about how she said home entertainment would boom. Once she stated it, I could already see how right she was going to be. There were already signs pointing in that direction, but it took her BPT viewpoint to make that vision clear. And she was right … about many of her predictions.

How do you find out about trends? BPTs need to stay aware of what is happening in the world.

- Twitter helps unearth trends.
- You can also set up an account at www.anderspink.com to curate trending ideas and content and find out more about what is going on in the world.
- Watching TED Talks are also a great way to stay on top of new ideas and trends. Download the TED app on your phone and incorporate a few TED talks into your life each week.
- Attend conferences in your field. This is a great way to meet people in your field, find out their concerns, problems, solutions, and a lot more. No matter what field you are in, conferences are an important way to stay connected to the big picture.

Understanding trends is important to reading the big picture. When I worked for a textbook publishing company back in the '90s, we knew that digital reading options were going to change things for publishers. This was the big picture. Books are still around, but without understanding the coming trend, the company would have had a rude surprise if it had not spent years of preparation and changes to accommodate the new digital world of publishing.

Imagine

TO ENVISION WHAT might be next, you must be open to new ideas and thoughts.

I love routines as much as the next person. In fact, I try to create routines to make my life less stressful, especially my morning routine when I am not fully awake. But you need to change your routines once in a while in order to unlock new discoveries.

Going for walks gets you away from your daily grind and allows you to free your mind a bit. It also creates that movement using both sides of the body that we discussed earlier. This is what happened to me when I took up running. Sometimes it takes the first few miles to sort out all the things in my head. At this point, my mind begins to wander freely and I get some great ideas and inspiration. That's just one of the many reasons people love running, and why people who have to stop running because of an injury are so upset about it.

I sometimes have trouble with my mind wandering in yoga class, when I'm supposed to be following what the teacher is saying. Yoga helps people get centered and let go of whatever is in the way of the expansion of their thoughts and it works well.

Preconceived notions often keep us from imagining new ideas and ways of doing things, and we tend to use past experiences to solve new problems. Sometimes our perception of what someone says or what happens is based on our own incorrect way of thinking. You'll miss a lot if you don't stay open to communicating with people and you judge them too quickly or based on what someone else said about them. Often a new product or idea comes from putting old ideas together in a different way, so stay open to new thoughts and by communicating openly with the people around you. Don't let past experiences limit you from thinking in new ways.

Let's use an example of a glass soft drink bottle. Other than storing a soft drink in it, and drinking out of it, try to name ten other uses for this bottle. Could you use a few bottles to prop up a shelf, or could you roll out clay or dough with it? What are some other uses for it?

Persevere

AFTER LEARNING ABOUT some different Big Picture Thinkers and their past experiences, and knowing that people aren't necessarily going to instantly recognize your great ideas as brilliant, even if they are brilliant,

Apply Big Picture Thinking Skills

you may have realized that having a bit of perseverance is going to be pretty useful.

I think we can all agree that Walt Disney was one of the great BPTs of all time. He was a dreamer and a doer, but he also had a glorious helping of perseverance. As Walt was quoted to say, "All the adversity I've had in my life, all my troubles and obstacles have strengthened me... You may not realize it when it happens, but a kick in the teeth may be the best thing in the world for you."

Walt not only had grand ideas and vision, but he also had the ability to translate his vision into reality, or so it seems. I don't have any specific evidence of this, but I speculate that it may be because right-brained Walt Disney partnered with his left-brained brother that he experienced whole brain success. Walt was known as the creative one with the ideas, and his brother Roy, was known as the businessman that handled the business side of things. Partnerships like theirs can work well to bring big ideas to successful fruition.

It can't be argued that Walt Disney knew the meaning of perseverance as he tried over and over to be successful. He spent every waking hour of every day working on his dreams, in spite of significant adversity in his life.

Walt was fired by the newspaper where he worked because he supposedly lacked creativity! He was so poor he had resorted to eating dog food. Walt spent his last few dollars on a train ticket to California to see if he could fare better somewhere else.

Walt nearly went bankrupt producing Snow White and the Seven Dwarfs, but he refused to give up, even mortgaging his own house to complete the film, which became one of the most popular films of 1937.

After numerous successes with his movies and cartoons, Walt set out to create a theme park that we all know as Disneyland. Disney World came later, which is a story in itself. This monumental project was part of his vision for EPCOT, the community of tomorrow. EPCOT was to be a revolution of urban planning.

When Disney died in 1966, the project was not complete, and without him to pursue his BPT vision, it became a different kind of theme park (but still a pretty cool one!). His brother Roy was still around to see the project to completion as a cool theme park.

There is much to be learned from this fabulous visionary. Luckily for us, he did not let failures keep him from trying again. Imagine what we would be missing without everything Walt Disney has provided for us to entertain us and show us what Big Picture Thinking can do for the world. Imagine what we would be missing without the business partnership with his brother, Roy, who helped this creative thinker turn his great visions into reality.

Think about where you are now, and how high your Crow's Nest would have to be to envision a project like Walt Disney World. That is BIG Picture Thinking at its best!

Your Training in a Nutshell

YOU MAY NOT be ready for a vision as big as Disney World or starting a societal movement. But, if you are, there is nothing stopping you from doing it. Begin wherever you are in your thinking and keep working towards the things that ignite your passion. Remember when you learned to drive? There were so many things to think about that you may have wondered if you would ever get the hang of it. And if you ever drove a stick shift, there were even more things to remember to do simultaneously.

But then as you practiced all these things, you eventually learned to do most of it without consciously thinking about it. You became aware of the slightest thing out of the ordinary, such as when that car looked like it was going to lurch out in front of you, and you slowed down or swerved to miss it. Other times, you may have arrived home from work and not really remembered any of the routine drive.

Learning takes place when the out of ordinary things occur. When we are not learning, we tend to stay in a sort of robotic, mindless state. We do what we know without engaging our minds in order to conserve our resources, and engage only to learn from what is new or different.

Big Picture Thinking requires mindfulness. You can train yourself to be mindful and observant. However, you must make a conscious choice to do so, or you will default to remembering only what jumps out in front of you. Engagement requires you to be motivated. Motivation and engagement will help you store the memories of the things you observe, so that you will be able to recall them later as clues when you are solving a puzzle of what is happening, or pursuing a vision of the future. Big Picture Thinking requires awareness of the past, present and the future. What becomes new is often not new, but a new combination of thoughts and ideas.

The brain stores memories into categories, with connections between the things that the brain determines to be similar. By strengthening both sides of your brain, you have an advantage of stronger connections between the visual and semantic versions of your knowledge, which helps you build the big picture more quickly in your mind.

Let's review the main points we have covered.

- Take a few steps back from the situation. Get up in the Crow's Nest view and look for the patterns and similarities of the "weeds."
- Become a keen observer. This provides you with the materials you need for thinking.
- Spend regular quiet time and practice focused thinking.
- Visit new places, meet new people and keep an eye on trends.
- Adopt optimism. Always look for the positive in every situation.
- Strengthen the skills on the less dominant side of your brain. Perform regular right or left-brain exercises.
- Perform activities that integrate the two hemispheres of your brain, such as walking, dancing, running or yoga.

Apply Big Picture Thinking Skills

- Be open to other people's viewpoints. Ask other people what they think and listen intentionally.
- Imagine the desired outcome. Once you have a vision of what the outcome looks like, you can start to see the steps that need to happen. When you have the big picture in mind, you can see how the day-to-day activities and the opportunities fit into it.
- Embrace thinking differently. Learn new things and adapt to the new big picture.
- Learn lessons in every experience. Everything is connected, and most experiences have a lesson that you can figure out.
- Spend time with other Big Picture Thinkers. Collaboration and verbalizing your ideas and observations with another can spark greater ideas and observations.

The brain needs nourishment, and a healthy diet is an important ingredient to thinking. Now you know an even better reason to eat healthy and exercise! Eat a healthy, nutritious diet to feed your brain, get enough sleep, and exercise to get your brain hemispheres working together.

You have all the pieces you need to become a Big Picture Thinker. If you need motivation, all you need to do is to read about any of the famous BPTs I mentioned in this book, or one of many that were not mentioned. Spend more time with the BPTs that you know personally.

BECOME A BIG PICTURE THINKER

There are many inspirational thinkers in the world that have shown us the path and the outcomes of some of their amazing work for inspiration. You are no different if you have the passion to make it happen! Good luck!

Other Books and Courses by Emily Nightingale

IF YOU ENJOYED this book, please consider these other books by Emily Nightingale.

The Successful Millennial:
Tips for Navigating the Corporate Jungle

More than 100 tips are provided to help you navigate more proficiently in the corporate workplace with colleagues and leaders, and become recognized for your expertise and style.

Get Promoted: Two Strategies That Work

Learn about the two most important strategies to help you get promoted.

Please visit skillshare.com (http://www.skillshare.com) and check out the video courses by Emily Nightingale.

Review Request

THANK YOU FOR taking the time to read this book. I hope you enjoyed it and found the information to be useful.

I would love to have your feedback, and would be grateful if you would post an honest review of the book. I love learning more about the reader's point of view. Your support and feedback does make a difference.

To leave a review, please visit *Become a Big Picture Thinker: Learn How to Think Big* book page on Amazon.com.

Scroll down to the Customer Reviews section. Locate the button labeled "Write a customer review" and click the button to enter your review.

Thank you in advance for your feedback!

Bibliography

"A Few Gifted Men Who Worked For Edison." *National Parks Service*, U.S. Department of the Interior, www.nps.gov/edis/learn/kidsyouth/the-gifted-men-who-worked-for-edison.htm.

"Are You a Big Picture Thinker or Detail-Oriented?" *The Fast Track*, www.quickbase.com/blog/are-you-a-big-picture-thinker-or-detail-oriented.

Balance, Brain. "Characteristics of a Left-Brained Child." *Home - Brain Balance Achievement Centers*, www.brainbalancecenters.com/blog/2014/07 characteristics-left-brained-child/.

Bono, Edward De. *Lateral Thinking: Creativity Step by Step*. Harper Perennial, 2015.

Brosseau, Denise. "What Is a Thought Leader?" What Is a Thought Leader? Thought Leadership Lab, n.d. Web. 15, July 2017.

By. "Why You Should Embrace The Power of Thinking Differently." *Personal Branding Blog - Stand Out In Your*

Career, 4 May 2016, www.personalbrandingblog.com/why-you-should-embrace-the-power-of-thinking-differently/.

Casto, Rae. "Activities for Enhancing the Right Brain." *LIVESTRONG.COM*, Leaf Group, 14 Aug. 2017, www.livestrong.com/article/130581-activities-enhancing-right-brain/.

"Characteristics of Left Brained People." *Career Trend*, careertrend.com/info-8312308-characteristics-left-brained-people.html.

"Concept Map." *Wikipedia*, Wikimedia Foundation, 14 Apr. 2018, en.wikipedia.org/wiki/Concept_map.

"Crow's Nest." *Wikipedia*, Wikimedia Foundation, 6 Jan. 2018, en.wikipedia.org/wiki/Crow's_nest.

Davis, Rebecca. "The Doctor Who Championed Hand-Washing And Briefly Saved Lives." *NPR*, NPR, 12 Jan. 2015, www.npr.org/sections/health-shots/2015/01/12/375663920/the-doctor-who-championed-hand-washing-and-saved-women-s-lives.

DiDuca, Michael. "Walt Disney ate dog food to survive - would you?" Linkedin..com. July 16, 2014. https://www.linkedin.com/pulse/20140716171434-71740143-walt-disney-ate-dog-food-to-survive-would-you/

Doepker, Derek. "Steve Jobs Systematically Cultivated His Creativity. You Can Too." *Entrepreneur*, 3 Aug. 2017, www.entrepreneur.com/article/297167.

Bibliography

"Edison and Ford Winter Estates." *Wikipedia*, Wikimedia Foundation, 3 Jan. 2018, en.wikipedia.org/wiki/Edison_and_Ford_Winter_Estates.

Edwards, Betty. *Drawing on the Right Side of the Brain*. Los Angeles, Ca.: Tarcher, 1989. Print.

Emerson, Chad, et al. *Project Future: the inside Story behind the Creation of Disney World*. Ayefour Publishing, 2010.

"Famous Diary Entries: Einstein Confesses His 'One Great Mistake.'" *Endpaper: The Paperblanks Blog*, Paperblanks Team, 12 Jan. 2018, blog.paperblanks.com/2013/03/famous-diary-entries-einstein-confesses-his-one-great-mistake/.

"Galileo." *Biography.com*, A&E Networks Television, 1 Aug. 2017, www.biography.com/people/galileo-9305220.

Grant, Adam M., and Sheryl Sandberg. *Originals: How Non-Conformists Change the World*. WH Allen, 2017.

H., Felix. "The Offbeat Habits of 7 Famous Leaders (Infographic)." *Lifehack*, Lifehack, 7 July 2017, www.lifehack.org/610515/the-offbeat-habits-of-7-famous-leaders-infographic-ap-pinterest-infographic?utm_content=bufferf7dd2.

"How to Integrate Your Right and Left Brain through Movement." *Sequence Wiz*, 8 Jan. 2015, sequencewiz.org/2014/08/13/integrating-right-and-left-brain/.

"Ignaz Semmelweis." *Wikipedia*, Wikimedia Foundation, 18 Apr. 2018, en.wikipedia.org/wiki/Ignaz_Semmelweis.

James Plafke on December 20, 2012 at 4:02 pm Comment. "Scientists Discover How Our Brains Categorize and Map Everything We See." *ExtremeTech*, 20 Dec. 2012, www.extremetech.com/extreme/143816-scientists-discover-how-our-brains-categorize-map.

Kendra Cherry | Reviewed by Steven Gans, MD. "Left Brain vs. Right Brain: The Surprising Truth." *Verywell*, www.verywell.com/left-brain-vs-right-brain-2795005.

Konnikova, Maria. *Mastermind: How to Think Like Sherlock Holmes*. Penguin Group, 2013.

"Leonardo Da Vinci." *Wikipedia*, Wikimedia Foundation, 6 Jan. 2018, en.wikipedia.org/wiki/Leonardo_da_Vinci.

"Linus Pauling." *Wikipedia*, Wikimedia Foundation, 22 Apr. 2018, en.wikipedia.org/wiki/Linus_Pauling.

"Martin Luther King Jr." *Wikipedia*, Wikimedia Foundation, 20 Apr. 2018, en.wikipedia.org/wiki/Martin_Luther_King_Jr.

Miller, Ashley. "How To Improve Your Right Brain." *LIVESTRONG.COM*, Leaf Group, 14 Aug. 2017, www.livestrong.com/article/192141-how-to-improve-your-right-brain/.

"Mind Mapping | Tony Buzan." *Tony Buzan RSS*, www.tonybuzan.com/about/mind-mapping/.

"Nicolaus Copernicus." *Biography.com*, A&E Networks Television, 28 Apr. 2017, www.biography.com/people/nicolaus-copernicus-9256984.

"Observation Exercises." *Study-Body-Language.com*, www.study-body-language.com/observation-exercise.html.

Paul. "10 Of the Most Multi-Talented People of All Time." *10Awesome.Com*, 16 Nov, 2015. 10awesome.com/10-of-the-most-multi-talented-people-of-all-time.

"Roy O. Disney." *Wikipedia*, Wikimedia Foundation, 7 Jan. 2018, en.wikipedia.org/wiki/Roy_O._Disney.

Santoso, Alex, et al. "10 Strange Facts About Einstein." *Neatorama*, www.neatorama.com/2007/03/26/10-strange-facts-about-einstein/.

"Semmelweis' Germ Theory." *The Introduction of Hand Washing*, explorable.com/semmelweis-germ-theory.

Sicinski, Adam. "How to Become a Visual Thinking Expert." *Visual Thinking Magic*, www.visualthinkingmagic.com/visual-thinking-expert.

Sicinski, Adam. "Visual Thinking and Pattern Recognition." *Visual Thinking Magic*, www.visualthinkingmagic.com/pattern-recognition.

Staff, GoodTherapy.org. "The Power of Positive Thinking: How to Change Your Viewpoint." *GoodTherapy.org Therapy Blog*, 6 Sept. 2016, www.

goodtherapy.org/blog/the-power-of-positive-thinking-how-to-change-your-viewpoint-0908168.

Stanet, Andrea. "Exercises to Stimulate the Left Side of the Brain." *LIVESTRONG.COM*, Leaf Group, 14 Aug. 2017, www.livestrong.com/article/343823-exercises-to-stimulate-the-left-side-of-the-brain/.

"Thomas Edison." *Biography.com*, A&E Networks Television, 4 Aug. 2017, www.biography.com/people/thomas-edison-9284349.

"What Is Leadership?" *Leadership Skills Training from MindTools.com*, www.mindtools.com/pages/article/newLDR_41.htm.

"Why Was Albert Einstein Considered Stupid?" *Albert Einstein and His Theories*, einsteinisamazing.weebly.com/why-was-albert-einstein-considered-stupid.html.

wikiHow. "How to Sharpen Your Powers of Observation." *WikiHow*, WikiHow, 1 Oct. 2017, www.wikihow.com/Sharpen-Your-Powers-of-Observation http://lifehacker.com/how-to-boost-your-observation-skills-and-learn-to-pay-a-1678229721.

Cover image from Pixabay.com. https://pixabay.com/en/bergdohle-jackdaw-winter-bird-3088224/ retrieved on April 21, 2018. CC0 Creative Commons license.

www.ingramcontent.com/pod-product-compliance
Lightning Source LLC
Chambersburg PA
CBHW071320040426
42444CB00009B/2055